GETTING TO KNOW THE WORLD'S GREATEST ARTISTS

JAMES MCNEILL
WHISTLER

WRITTEN AND ILLUSTRATED BY MIKE VENEZIA

CHILDREN'S PRESS®
A DIVISION OF SCHOLASTIC INC.
NEW YORK TORONTO LONDON AUCKLAND SYDNEY
MEXICO CITY NEW DELHI HONG KONG
DANBURY, CONNECTICUT

Cover: *Arrangement in Grey and Black No. 1, Portrait of the Artist's Mother,* by James Abbott McNeill Whistler. 1871, oil on canvas, 144.3 x 162.5 cm. © Bridgeman Art Library International Ltd., London/New York/ Musée d'Orsay, Paris, France.

Colorist for illustrations: Dave Ludwig

Library of Congress Cataloging-in-Publication Data

Venezia, Mike.
 James McNeill Whistler / written and illustrated by Mike Venezia.
    p. cm.— (Getting to know the world's greatest artists)
Summary: Describes the life and work of the American-born painter who spent much of his life abroad.
 ISBN 0-516-22578-2 (lib. bdg.) 0-516-26978-X (pbk.)
 1. Whistler, James McNeill, 1834-1903—Juvenile literature. 2.
Artists—United States—Biography—Juvenile literature. [1. Whistler,
James McNeill, 1834-1903. 2. Artists.] I. Title. II. Series.
 N6537.W4V46 2004
 759.13—dc21
                      2003000014

CHILDREN'S PRESS and associated logos are trademarks
and or registered trademarks of Scholastic Library Publishing.
SCHOLASTIC and associated logos are trademarks and or
registered trademarks of Scholastic Inc.

1 2 3 4 5 6 7 8 9 10 R 12 11 10 09 08 07 06 05 04 03

James McNeill Whistler was born in Lowell, Massachusetts, in 1834. Aside from being a great artist, Whistler was known for his clever sense of humor and flashy appearance. James Whistler always wanted to be noticed. He even had a white curl on top of his head that stood out from the rest of his black hair.

The Artist in his Studio, by James Abbott McNeill Whistler. 1865-66, oil on paper mounted on panel, 62.9 x 46.4 cm. © Art Institute of Chicago, Friends of American Art Collection, 1912.141.

San Biagio, Venice, by James Abbott McNeill Whistler. 1879-80, etching and drypoint printed in dark brown ink on wove paper, 20.5 x 30.5 cm. © Bridgeman Art Library International Ltd., London/New York/Agnew & Sons, London.

James McNeill Whistler was considered one of the most rebellious artists of his time. Today, there doesn't seem to be anything especially shocking or different about his paintings and prints.

During the late 1800s, though, many of Whistler's simple, dreamy scenes seemed much too abstract for people's tastes.

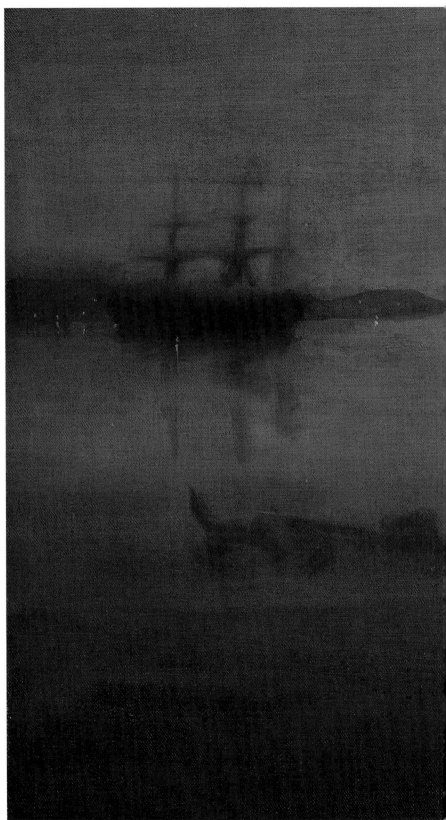

Nocturne in Blue and Silver:
The Lagoon, Venice, by James
Abbott McNeill Whistler. 1879-80,
oil on canvas, 50.16 x 65.4 cm.
© Museum of Fine Arts, Boston,
Emily L. Ainsley Fund; 42.302.

James McNeill Whistler had a very interesting childhood. When he was nine years old, his family moved to St. Petersburg, Russia. James's father, a construction engineer, was asked to help build a railroad there.

St. Petersburg was a magnificent city. It was filled with royal buildings, cathedrals, palaces, and museums. The emperor of Russia, Czar Nicholas I, made sure there were parties, operas, concerts, and fireworks going on all the time.

United States Military Song of the Graduates cover, by James Abbott McNeill Whistler. 1852, lithograph. © Art Institute of Chicago, Walter S. Brewster Collection, 1933.281.

Dress Parade: Sketches; part of ALBUM, by James Abbott McNeill Whistler. c. 1852. © Metropolitan Museum of Art, Gift of Margaret C. Buell, Helen L. King, and Sybil A. Walk, 1970, (1970.121.18-19).

James Whistler got a good education in St. Petersburg. His parents noticed that he had an unusual talent for drawing, and sent him to the best art school in Russia. The Whistlers lived in St. Petersburg until, sadly, Mr. Whistler died. In 1849, the family moved back to the United States.

When James was sixteen, his mother decided
he should enroll at the United States Military
Academy at West Point. James's father had
gone to the same school. James wasn't the best
military student, though. He was known as a
prankster. The only class he did well in was
drawing. After three years at West Point,
James was asked to leave.

Etching, *Sketches on the Coast Survey Plate,* by James Abbott McNeill Whistler. c. 1854, etching on paper, 14.5 x 25.9 cm. © Freer Gallery of Art, Smithsonian Institution, Washington, D.C., Gift of Charles Lang Freer, F1897.17.

After James Whistler left West Point, he got a job in the drawing division of the Coastal Survey Department in Washington, D.C. It was Whistler's job to copy maps onto copper plates, or sheets. This was done so that maps could be printed in large numbers. These types of prints are called etchings.

James loved learning about and making etchings. When he became bored copying maps, James sometimes added his own drawings and doodles to make things more interesting.

Ile de la Cite of Paris, by Felix Benoist. 1860, engraving.
© Art Resource, NY/Bibliotheque Nationale, Paris, France.

It's not surprising that James Whistler's job at the survey department didn't last very long. James didn't care, though. He had now made up his mind to be an artist! James Whistler decided to study art in the world's greatest art center at the time—Paris, France.

He left the United States in 1855, never to return. Instead of spending his small amount of money wisely, James bought the fanciest outfit he could afford. James Whistler wanted to make a big splash when he arrived in Paris.

James Whistler enjoyed Paris. He met
other artists, took art classes, and visited art
museums. He started making lots of etchings.
James also began to spend time in another
great art city, London, England. He had an
older married sister who lived there.

In London,
James saw busy
dock areas along
the famous Thames
river. Even though

Wapping, by James Abbott McNeill Whistler. 1861-64, oil on canvas, 72.0 x 101.8 cm.
© National Gallery of Art, Washington, D.C., John Hay Whitney Collection.

they were some of the most run-down, scary, and dangerous neighborhoods in London, they caught James's attention. He felt that the shapes of crumbling old buildings, ships with webs of masts and rigging, and dark alleyways were all beautiful in their own way.

The Last Evening, by James Jacques Joseph Tissot. 1873, oil on canvas, 72.4 x 102.8 cm.
© Bridgeman Art Library International Ltd., London/New York/Guildhall Art Gallery,
Corporation of London, UK.

The scenes Whistler started etching and painting were very different from what people were used to seeing. When James started out as an artist, everyone expected paintings to be carefully done with lots of details. They especially wanted pictures that told a story, like the one above.

As Whistler developed his work, he became convinced that paintings and etchings could simply be beautiful colors and well-positioned shapes that are pleasing to look at. He thought the worst reason to paint a picture was to tell a story. He also hated the idea of cluttering his artwork with lots of fussy details.

The Ocean, by James Abbott McNeill Whistler. 1866, oil on canvas, 80.7 x 101.9 cm.
© The Frick Collection, New York.

In order to make his own artwork as beautiful and pleasing to look at as possible, Whistler looked to a number of different artists for inspiration. He enjoyed the everyday scenes of French artist Gustave Courbet. Whistler also really liked Japanese and Chinese prints. He felt that their strong shapes, simple colors, and flat backgrounds came together to create perfect pictures.

Nocturne in Grey and Gold: Chelsea Snow, by James Abbott McNeill Whistler. 1876, oil on canvas, 46.4 x 62.9 cm. © Bridgeman Art Library International Ltd., London/ New York/Fogg Art Museum, Harvard University Art Museums, USA, Bequest of Grenville L. Winthrop.

James Whistler worked hard over the years experimenting and combining ideas he learned from different artists. He eventually discovered his own very original style of art.

Variations of Flesh Colour and Green - The Balcony, by James Abbott McNeill Whistler. 1864-70, oil on wood panel, 61.4 x 48.8 cm. © Freer Gallery of Art, Smithsonian Institution, Washington, D.C., Gift of Charles Lang Freer, F1892.23.

21

One of the first paintings Whistler did in his new style was a portrait of his girlfriend. It was called *Symphony in White, No.1: The White Girl.* This painting got a lot of attention at a big art show in Paris. Unfortunately, the attention it got was pretty bad. *The White Girl* seemed to shock everyone who saw it. People wanted to know why the girl was wearing a casual flowing dress instead of a decorative gown. They wanted to know why her hair wasn't done up in a fancy style, and why the background didn't give some idea of what her house was like. Most of all, they wanted to know why Whistler's brush strokes were so sloppy and rough.

Symphony in White, No. 1: The White Girl, by James Abbott McNeill Whistler. 1862, oil on canvas, 213 x 107.9 cm. © National Gallery of Art, Washington, D.C., Harris Whittemore Collection, photo by Richard Carafelli.

Symphony in White, No. III, by James Abbott McNeill Whistler. 1865-67, oil on canvas, 51.4 x 76.9 cm. © Bridgeman Art Library International Ltd., London/New York/The Barber Institute of Fine Arts, University of Birmingham.

But Whistler's *White Girl* was exactly what he wanted it to be. It was a beautiful picture of a girl that was pleasing to look at. It didn't make any difference to him that no one knew who the girl was or what kind of life she lived.

To make his point even clearer, Whistler used a musical term in the painting's name. He gave many of his paintings musical titles, such as *Symphony, Harmony,* or *Variation.* Whistler felt that his paintings were kind of like music for your eyes. He also stopped signing his work. Instead, he began to use a butterfly design to identify his pictures.

Harmony in Grey and Green: Miss Cecily Alexander, by James Abbott McNeill Whistler. 1872, oil on canvas, 190 x 98.7 cm. © Art Resource, NY/Tate Gallery, London, UK.

Arrangement in Grey and Black No. 1, Portrait of the Artist's Mother, by James Abbott McNeill Whistler. 1871, oil on canvas, 144.3 x 162.5 cm. © Bridgeman Art Library International Ltd., London/New York/ Musée d'Orsay, Paris, France.

One of the world's most famous paintings is Whistler's portrait of his mother. The proper name of the painting is *Arrangement in Grey and Black No. 1, Portrait of the Artist's Mother.* Whistler loved his mother very much, but in this painting he was mostly interested in bringing attention to the arrangement of strong shapes and few, perfect colors.

Nocturne in Blue and Gold, Old Battersea Bridge, by James Abbott McNeill Whistler. 1872-1875, oil on canvas, 68.3 x 51.2 cm. © Art Resource, NY/Tate Gallery, London, UK.

Another word Whistler used for some of his paintings was *Nocturne,* which means "nighttime." Whistler loved the way rivers, harbors, and cities looked in the evening. Some of his most beautiful, moody paintings are nighttime scenes.

Once, a famous art critic insulted one of Whistler's *Nocturne* paintings. It was the fireworks scene on the next page. The critic thought Whistler was a sloppy, no-good artist. He wrote that the painting was like "flinging a pot of paint in the public's face."

James Whistler was angry and hurt. He decided to sue the critic, John Ruskin, for libel—making unfair statements that ruin a person's reputation.

This was an important case for Whistler and for the history of art. During the court case, James Whistler explained his ideas about art and defended his right to make the kinds of paintings he was making. The judge ended up agreeing with Whistler.

Nocturne in Black and Gold, the Falling Rocket, by James Abbott McNeill Whistler. 1875, oil on panel, 60.2 x 46.7 cm. © Bridgeman Art Library International Ltd., London/New York/The Detroit Institute of Arts, USA, Gift of Dexter M. Ferry Jr.

The Rialto, by James Abbott McNeill Whistler. 1880, etching and drypoint, 29.3 x 20 cm. © Art Resource, NY/Sotheby Parke-Bernet, Editorial Photocolor Archives.

Even though James Whistler won his court case, he had spent so much money on the lawsuit that he was almost broke. Fortunately, right at this time, James was asked to make a series of etchings and pastel drawings of Venice, Italy. In 1879, James Whistler traveled to Venice, where he made some of his best etchings ever.

The Storm - Sunset, by James Abbott McNeill Whistler. 1880, pastel on brown wove paper, 18.4 x 28.6 cm. © Bridgeman Art Library International Ltd., London/New York/Fogg Art Museum, Harvard University, Cambridge, MA, USA, Bequest of Grenville L. Winthrop.

When he returned to London, Whistler was able to sell lots of his new masterpieces. His ideas about art slowly began to catch on. For the rest of his life, Whistler did pretty well financially.

Bead Stringers, by James Abbott McNeill Whistler. 1879-80, crayon and pastel on golden-brown paper, 27.6 x 11.7 cm. © Freer Gallery of Art, Smithsonian Institution, Washington, D.C., Gift of Charles Lang Freer, F1905.124.

James McNeill Whistler died in London, England, in 1903. He spent his life not only creating remarkable works of art, but convincing people that there was more than one way to look at, and appreciate, art.

Arrangement in Grey: Portrait of the Painter, by James Abbott McNeill Whistler. 1872, oil on canvas, 74.9 x 53.3 cm. © Bridgeman Art Library International Ltd., London/New York/The Detroit Institute of Arts, USA, Gift of Henry Glover Stevens.

The works of art in this book can be seen at the following places:

The Art Institute of Chicago
The Barber Institute of Fine Arts, University of Birmingham
The British Museum, London
The Detroit Institute of Arts
Fogg Art Museum, Cambridge
Freer Gallery of Art, Smithsonian Institution, Washington, D.C.

The Frick Collection, New York
Hunterian Art Gallery, University of Glasgow
Metropolitan Museum of Art, New York
Musée d'Orsay, Paris
Musée Fabre, Montepellier, France
Museum of Fine Arts, Boston
National Gallery of Art, Washington, D.C.
Tate Gallery, London